John Wickliffe Ricks

Cuttings

John Wickliffe Ricks

Cuttings

ISBN/EAN: 9783337868833

Printed in Europe, USA, Canada, Australia, Japan

Cover: Foto ©Andreas Hilbeck / pixelio.de

More available books at **www.hansebooks.com**

CUTTINGS

BY

MRS. JOHN WICKLIFFE RICKS,

AUTHOR OF "WELDED LINKS."

PRICE. FIFTY CENTS.

SAN FRANCISCO:

BACON & COMPANY, BOOK AND JOB PRINTERS,

Clay Street, corner of Sansome.

1877.

Cuttings:

BY

MRS. JOHN WICKLIFFE RICKS,

AUTHOR OF "WELDED LINKS."

PRICE, FIFTY CENTS.

SAN FRANCISCO:

BACON & COMPANY, BOOK AND JOB PRINTERS,

Clay Street, corner of Sansome.

1877.

DEDICATION.

With unfaltering faith in the universal love of God, whose mercy to His children " endureth forever," I most lovingly dedicate "Cut-tings " to the memory of those brave Reformers, who, ignoring personal glory and regardless of the emoluments of fame, have labored earnestly for the promotion of truth and the advancement of that which pertains to the interests of mankind.

Mrs. JOHN WICKLIFFE RICKS.

San Francisco, December, 1876.

CONTENTS.

———

CUTTINGS.

DESTINY.

Destiny is a spreading out on the canvas of time the untwisted conceptions of God's purposes, which have been inlaid in the magnetic cable of eternal thought, to be separated into knots and skeins, as warp and woof on the reel of eternity, and from thence to be woven in the mystic shuttles of Irresistible Will, to be wound in the loom of Incomparable Majesty into faultless fabrics with which to clothe the perfection of illimitable works. The tapestry of mortal life, the adornments of earth and sky, the glory of angels, the bliss of saints, are but the inimitable patterns of the Almighty's design, transferred to the objects for which they were designed. The developments of each day, both in time and eternity, are but the results of the unfoldments of the Almighty's purpose, liberated from the girdle which encompasses Divine will. Who shall stay the Lord's intent, or who subvert His mighty plan? The various manifestations presented for human observation, are as natural a sequence as the cycle of changing seasons. Time is the mighty power which unrolls the coil wherein is deposited the hidden intents of the Lord. The people which are yet to walk this earth; the statesmen which are to manipulate the affairs of nations yet unborn; the orators, poets and scholars who are to electrify human intelligence in the centuries which lie folded back in the swaddling clothes of God's intent, live in the chemical processes of the Almighty, as veritably as do they whose quickened pulses speed them on to the unknown. The revolutions of day and night, the changing seasons, the fall of rain, summer's heat and winter's snow, spring-time and harvest, the rushing into life of animate nature, and the created beauties of a vast creation, are but the letting out of the illimitable sail which is reefed in the mechanical skill of Omnipotence. Creation has not been the subject of chance, neither was disorder brought out of chaos. Everything has developed in harmony, showing a fitness of each for the adaptability of that which should come after. The creations of to-day are the foundations upon which the morrow builds its edifice ; so in the untold decade of centuries, each has builded its pyramid of colossal progress upon the dome of its predecessor, each reaching nearer and still nearer the perfection of its antetype.

MEMORY.

Memory is the canvas sheet of the soul, upon which are outspread an imperishable panorama of all the devices which the mind has conjectured or the spirit conceived. It is the talisman of the past, and the exchequer whose tribunal shall justly adjudge the unfoldings of the great scroll of life. The paint of excuse, mixed with the oil of repentance and the grief of despair, may not obliterate one trace which the brush of thought has stereotyped on this magnetic scroll.

Its cartoons are as varied as have been the flights of thought, the conceptions of imagination, the acts of life, or the pictures presented in the spiritual, intellectual, moral, affectional or physical of human experience. She takes the canvas sheet of the soul, fresh from nature's own hand, and writes upon its surface the sentiments and passions of the human heart. She unrolls her canvas sheet on which earth and sky are painted, so that the mind can examine all the hues and forms of sensible things in its impressions of the past. She sends her telegrams beyond the tomb and brings us messages from eternity, from those whom we first loved, in their happiest moods and sweetest expressions. She sees them rise above the agonies of dissolution, and gives us back our cherished ones in the loveliest forms they wore. She sends her messages back to the green of her earliest gambols, and pushing her electric wires through the vault, bridges over the boundary of time, and brings light from eternity. She triumphs on the wings of faith, and paints a roadway to glory. Uniting her canvas with that of past ages, she scales the ladder of history, and runs down the pages of its unfoldings, inweaving their record into her own sublime canvas. The cobwebs of time may dim its texture and throw a shadow over its pictures, but the brush of eternity shall make radiant every cartoon upon its surface, and bring them out with renewed splendor. It shall be the mansion through which the disenthralled spirit may roam at will, gathering fresh blossoms from the germs of thought, which budded on the canvas of life, to reap their full fruition in the sunshine of immortality. Being *en rapport* with those who have passed on ages before, she links the canvas of mortality to that of celestial order, and weaves the fabric of time and that of eternity into one scroll, while she follows rapidly the unfoldings of the great mystical cable of eternity, as God unlooses the coils from the hand of His Imperial Majesty, giving to man the scope of the past, present and future as a field for his explorations. In this "house of many mansions," its treasures shall forever multiply, imparting to translated souls a restful labor which shall yield a harvest of perpetual joys, and an eternity of new delights.

MAN.

From the circle of revolving cycles swung out into active conscious existence by the pendulum of eternal thought, came forth man as the outgrowth of Divine wisdom and beneficence, being the positive creation of Infinity, brought upon the arena of life in juxtaposition to God, having received his spirit fresh from the breath of the Almighty, bearing the Divine impress as a seal of kinship, and an heir to immortality; he raises above the physical of his being a superstructure lasting as is eternity, inwrought with the embellishments of a crowned intellectuality, and a burnished spirituality in which the Godhead is typified; he is joined to Infinity by the link of immortality, and is allied to God by reason of spiritual assimilation, and a mental capacity for unraveling the principles inwrought in the combination of elements which form the unity and harmony of God's mysterious laws. Growing up into the full stature of manhood by the unity of his spiritual and intellectual nature, he untwists the riddle of life ; by the application of his soul unto wisdom, associated with his intellectual unfoldment he wears the signet of the Infinite upon his brow, and becomes the associate of the purified, and with them walks in the light, and takes sweet counsel of God. He discerns the tides of life, and so gauges its streams by healthful exercise and proper nutrition as to preserve the equilibrium of the body to the full measure of its appointed years. By judicious discipline and care of the mental, he becomes capable of traversing realms of thought where nought but elements containing principles of Godhood may tarry. By his spiritual clairaudient susceptibility he catches messages wafted from spirit-land, giving him assurance of the life which is to come ; and he triumphs in the promises of immortality which are inscribed within the volumes of his own soul. Unfolding their pages, one by one, he becomes en rapport with the harmonies of God's earthly temple, and there holds communings with seraphims whose harmonious songs reverberate through earth and sky. Wisdom and mercy have their habitations in this purified mansion ; there the lamps of God are ever kept burning, rendering the otherwise night of the soul luminous as the day. The flaming swords of purity ever guard the gates of that structure, that nothing which defiles may enter therein. Of all created earthly intelligences, man is the only one with an organization compounded of such parts that, being in perfect harmony with himself, he can catch the influences from without, and determine with accuracy the nature of the spiritual, intellectual, mental and moral condition of those with whom he comes in contact, becoming in fact a highly sensitive psychological scale, to enter whose presence is to throw off the gossamer web which conceals the human character from the gaze of those whose only province it is to see material things through the natural vision.

These psychologic gifts, though inherent in man, are less frequently brought into requisition than any other element in his nature, although being of the utmost importance to guide him in his daily transactions of life, yet are they known less of than the minor laws which pertain to the sustenance of the body ; nor will they have their full unfoldment in man until the spiritual and intellectual are inthroned as umpire of head and heart, thus forming a perfect, harmonious trinity of soul, body and intellect. Man thus attuned has the windows of his soul opened, and light comes streaming in upon his spiritual vision, direct from God, the good Father of all intelligences; permeating, enriching and purifying his entire nature, so that he is enabled to behold spiritual and intellectual beauties, and trace them in their rich unfoldments as readily as he does the charms which are presented to his outer or bodily vision. Man thus illuminated is not altogether the subject of circumstances : he works out the development of his own character, having first put himself in a condition by which the good Father works through him to do His good pleasure. Being thus disciplined, he is in accord with God, moving in spiritual harmony to the Divine will, and becomes receptive to the teachings of angelic agencies, by which God has ordained to bring men unto Himself. God and humanity are one grand body, of which God is the heart and brain, mankind being the members. Intelligence is the nerve-work of this grand structure, and like the human system, that which affects the remotest part, the brain instantly takes cognizance of. So it is, the intelligence of "a sparrow shall not fall to the ground without your Father's" notice. By reason of the superiority of man's intelligence, he is lifted to an exalted position in this intellectual mesh-work of nerve; and whatever affects him, be he Hindoo, Mussulman, Pagan or Christian, sends a thrill to the responsive heart of the universal Father, calling attention to the child He has created, to a member of His complex, yet merciful system. Hence it is that the thought of man triumphs over space, and his soul-petitionings reach the ear of the Almighty. Man walking in the dignity of his intellectual, spiritual and moral strength, has a soul affiliation to God, and is in communion with Him "by whom and through whom all things exist." Man is not left unto himself alone, aided only by sight and reason. The good Father addresses Himself to-day to the understanding of man through the spirituality of his nature, by convoy of seen and unseen angels, as veritably as he spake to Balaam in the valley of Pethor. Numbers: Chap. 22; verses 22 to 35 inclusive. And His mighty love to man is none the less now, than when He opened the spiritual eyes of the Prophet that he might see "the angel of the Lord standing in the way." And men even now have sore occasion to say to the angel as did Balaam : " I have sinned, in that I knew not that thou stoodest in the way against me." " The mercy of the Lord endureth forever," and " His hand is not shortened that it can

not save," through the agencies of His divine appoint-
ing. We are indebted to the ministrations of angels
for the wise teachings of Paul. Had he not, by the
Spirit of Christ, been arrested on his way to Damascus,
and his soul vision opened, would he not have con-
tinued to persecute the saints, honestly supposing that
he was doing God's service? The human mind is
spiritually blind until God touches the windows of the
soul, and aids reason by the illuminating influences of
His own divine Spirit. Let not man frequent the habitations of vice, nor walk in the counsel of the ungodly,
if he would have it possible for angels to minister to
his spiritual necessities. Though the shackles of
bondage were to fall from his loosed spirit, and the
prison gates of his soul were all unbarred, and his
inner life made radiant with divine glory, yet the fre-
quency of sin shall forge chains from which the interposition of God's mercy shall alone be able to wrest the
reimprisoned spirit. Of all the mechanism of God's
vast creation, there is nothing so sensitive as the magnetic touch of the human soul. The least of all its
tendrils,when moved upon by outward influences, sends
a reverberatory thrill to the minutest part of its deli-
cate yet indestructible structure. And *this* is the *real*
man, the physical, being the mere outer covering of
this imperishable edifice. Every being who lives is
his or her own master mechanic, building up from the
base soul a furnished habitation,which shall survive the
wastes of time, and, rising above the dissolution of the
mortal, shall rear its ethereal temple to the honor of
immortal glory, or the threatening dangers of humili-
ation and despair.

NATURE'S OFFERING.

Where the leaves shall talk together,
　　And the answering waters sigh,
Where all nature joins the choral,
　　Tiny insect, buzzing fly.

Where the flowers ope their petals,
　　Looking upward to the sky,
In their face of wondrous beauty
　　Offer incense—well as I.

And the lowing of the cattle
　　Answering to the call amain,
And the heifer by the brooklet
　　As she joins in the refrain,

In her neck stretched out and upward,
　　In her meek and wistful eye,
Worship God in every impulse,
　　Well as you, oh! saint, or I.

Nature all joins in the anthem,
　　Sings a song least understood;
There's no offering half so ample
　　As the wild primeval wood.

Sings she in her leafy branches,
　　Sings she in her clustering vines,
Offers worship in the zephyrs,
　　Whispering through majestic pines.

There the silver-luted songsters
　　Sing their vestal hymns of praise,

And their worship is as grateful
As the Psalmist's sweetest lays.

And the poor unlettered red-men
Wandering in ancestral wood,
Have communings with the Father,
With the spirit of all good.

In the innocence of childhood,
In the unheard breath of prayer,
In the silent tear of sorrow
Dwells the Lord God even there.

HOPE.

Like the roseate hue of morning's proudest Aurora,
Hope paints her gilded offering on the panoply of the
soul, adorning it with those charms and graces which
render life an ambrosial bower, whose sweet fragrance
dispenses its generous benefactions on all who come
within the radius of its sweet perfume. She crowns
the mountain tops of the heart's loftiest aspirations,
and writes upon their crests with the pencil's richest
drapery the embellishments of her fairest promises.
She lights up the world with the halo of her glory.
To the lone mariner she is his polar star, his beacon
light. She lights up the darkness of the dungeon
and gives a radiance of glory in the gloom of despair.
To the orphan in the desolation of his lonely musings,
she is his companion and sweet comforter. To the
distressed in every sphere of life, she is the panacea

for all their sorrows, and a balm for every contrite spirit. She pierces the darkest vaults of death, clothes with imperial robes of trust and confidence the trembling soul in its exit to the unknown, and points the departing spirit in its new arena of life, safe to the haven of triumphant rest in the bosom of its God.

ENVY.

Unsavory as bitter waters, rayless as the vaults of the tomb, cold as the Stygian river: such is the soul, whose radius encircles and fosters the foul spirit of envy or revenge. Hissing serpents crawl within its charnel-house—and the poison of the Upas issues from its tongue.

Like the forked lightning, laden with the missiles of death, it strikes at its unsuspecting victim in the day of its brightest glory, when there is not a cloud on the canopy of the soul to give warning of its approach. The roll of thunder carried far and wide on the barbed tongue of scandal, is the chariot of its armor bearer.

From the fragrance of sweetest flowers it culls noxious vapors, and from the brightest effulgence proceeding from the luminous orb of a pure spirit and a bright intellectuality, its dwarfed heart only feels the withering blight of the night-shade. On the perfection of beauty it reflects its own hideousness. From nature's exhaustless laboratory of fruit and flowers, healing streams, and cooling shades, it gathers nought but bitter herbs. It shakes hands only with darkness, and fattens in the valley of Death, on the bleached bones of its own victims. Its garments are tattered rags, torn from vestal robes with which to cover its own hideousness, and it reeks with the slain of its own despoilation. It forced its way into Paradise, and witnessing the more perfect estate of God's later creation, seduced the brain of Adam by the fragile form of the woman, thus reducing the generation of men to servitude all the days of their life. It was envy which stung the ungenerous heart of Cain into animosity against his more favored brother, and sent the stainless soul of Abel, perched on an angel's wing, into Heaven. The envy of Haman placed himself upon the gallows which he had prepared for another, murdered ten of his sons, and slaughtered seventy and seven thousand of his kindred, while it removed the sackcloth and ashes from the suppliant form of his intended victim, rescued from destruction a mighty people, and clothing Mordecai in royal apparel, placed him next unto King Ahasuerus. It was revenge which put the head of John the Baptist into a charger and gave it into the keeping of a strange woman. An envy as base as that which released the soul of the first martyr, put the head of the beautiful Mary, Queen of Scots, to the block, while sister angels draped in spotless robes, bending over her quivering form, veiled their faces in sorrow at the act which sent her pure spirit to the throne of God.

The venerable age of this Heaven-abhorred culprit, renders not its crimes less pernicious than were its atrocities in the earlier days of its youth. It requires a magnanimity of heart equal to that which caused the utterance of the ever memorable words, " With malice toward none and charity for all," to look with commiseration on those who are addicted to the indulgence of its malign influence. To enable humanity to excuse the crime of this offence, an individual must be possessed of a spirit of generosity and long forbearance, like unto that which indited the incomparable prayer, uttered in the dying throes of the Crucified, "Father, forgive them, they know not what they do," and to give expression to that other prayer: "Forgive us our trespasses as we forgive them who trespass against us"; and not to have the answering of the petition bring maledictions on the suppliant's head, one must possess a spirit of forgiveness like unto that of a God.

TRUTH.

"Clear as the sun, fair as the moon, and terrible as an army with banners," such in epitome is Truth (the Queen of Heaven). In her fair form is embodied all the charms with which the Great Artificer has decorated His mighty universe. In her divine presence the graces of the Pleiades would pale in their spotless lustre; and in their translation to Heaven find a rival far excelling in beauty, form, and grace, anything which their loftiest imagination could picture, or the brush of an Archangel could paint. She dwells in the humble dew-drop, and trails her spotless robe uncontaminated alike through vast prairies of sweet-scented flowers, o'er the hazy dome of Heaven's faultless arch, and through the slime, scum, and purlieus of sin-besotted cities.

2

In the magnitude of her proportions she environs the infinity of space.

She rides upon the winged lightning, and makes her chariot the Universe. Her voice is heard alike in the sublime and awe-inspiring roar of Heaven's artillery, and in the musical flow of Ocean's inimitable cadences. She speaks her mute language from stony cliffs, from arid wastes, from ocean's depths, and heaven's eternal dome. Her standard-bearer is the law of infinity, written alike upon the tiniest insect upon which our unconscious tread crushes out its meagre functions of life, as upon the incomparable bow of Jehovah's promise suspended in the air.

With the index finger of Nature's indisputable law, she points to her fair proportions, gracing the traversed and untraversed vaults of the eternal blue.

She descends into the depth of ocean, and paints her roseate hue, such as a god might envy, upon coral reefs, and upon the sea's closeted offerings. On Shasta's towering height, as upon each trembling blade of grass, she has affixed her signet ; and, crowning all the mysterious mechanism of humanity, is the central pivot upon which she has placed her greatest glory, and endowed it with her richest beneficent gifts. She was the light that went forth at the fiat of Jehovah·in creation's early dawn, and her radiance illuminates wherever God has spoke creation into life. She is kind, though imperative ; generous, yet unforgiving. In her there is no "variableness, neither shadow of turning." Compensation is her just award. "In the day that thou eatest thereof, thou shalt surely die," was the irrevocable fiat that went forth to those who should break her immutable laws.

Her symmetrical form encompasses the boundaries of time, and is the panoply that infolds Jehovah, and the magnitude of His incomparable works. At her behest the tides obey, and revolving worlds, like marshaled hosts, in the endless rounds of their circuitous journey, obey her mandates; while the Infinite is the fountain-head from whence issues all her divergent streams.

NOTHING BUT ASHES.

Nothing but ashes!
The roses decay—
Their beautiful bloom
Soon fades away
And leaves
Nothing but ashes.

Nothing but ashes!
Oh! memory, how sweet
It's mystical charms
Is laid at our feet
And yields
Nothing but ashes.

Nothing but ashes!
And is there no rest
For wearisome care
Which rankles the breast,
And leaves
Nothing but ashes?

Nothing but ashes
　For hopes and for fears,
For joys and sorrows
　Which make up our years,
　　Is there
Nothing but ashes?

Nothing but ashes
　On which to recline?
For famishing hearts
　And souls that repine,
　　Is there
Nothing but ashes?

Nothing but ashes
　For prodigal son?
Or Magdalen's heart,
　Which anguish has wrung,
　　Is there
Nothing but ashes?

Nothing but ashes!
　Has memory's chain
No link which exists
　Beyond this refrain?
　　Is life
Nothing but ashes?

Nothing but ashes
　On which to bridge o'er
The dark flowing strand
　To Eternity's shore?
　　Is there
Nothing but ashes?

Nothing but ashes!
  Life's roseate hue
Fades on the lips—
  Is subtle as dew,
    And leaves
Nothing but ashes.

Nothing but ashes!
  And is there no charm
Which shall the dark tomb
  Of terror disarm?
    Is there
Nothing save ashes?

Nothing but ashes!
  The Crown and the Cross—
Shall these be accounted
  As idle as dross,
    Which yield
Nothing but ashes?

Nothing but ashes?
  Yes! Infinite love—
A Father's compassion—
  Which flows from above,
    Will yield
Something save ashes.

HAPPINESS DEFINED.

Should I take the wings of the morning, circuiting the uttermost parts of the earth; should I traverse the boundaries of time, or delve into the secret chambers of Infinity; should I hold converse with the gods, and chant with the choirs of the Seraphims, still in none of these may I find the priceless gem for which the heart ever pants, and for which millions, now consigned back to the bosom of earth, lie vanquished in their pursuit after the priceless boon. Nor yet, with all life's busy throng, replete with its budding hope, and fragrant with the incense of the soul's loftiest inspirations, nor yet perched upon the giddy pinnacle of fame, ablaze with the world's homage, shall this jewel of greatest price be found. So great its virtues, so rare the gem, that but few are ever able to wear it emblazoned upon the shield of the soul. And yet its possibilities are within the reach of nearly the entire human family. Would you possess this treasure of rarest price : go down into the inner temple of the soul—into the " holy of holies " of man's nature, and set that inner sanctuary fully in order, as did the Master drive out the money changers, and everything which believeth and maketh a lie; and there in that inner temple, in its holiest sanctuary, may this rarest gem be found—a free gift fresh from the hand of a beneficent Father, sitting there as umpire over head and heart, dispensing blessings which crowned heads might envy, and at which, in rapt admiration, angels might wonder and adore. In the harmony of our own nature is to be found this priceless boon (happiness). Its growth is eternal, its storehouse exhaustless, its resources wide as the universe. 'Tis the river of life, which flows in healing streams through the city of humanity's soul, making glad all who lave in its placid waters.

Cast Your Bread Upon the Waters.

Cast your bread upon the waters,
   They are winding to the sea,
And with human souls are freighted—
   Destined for eternity.

Cast your bread upon the waters—
   Sow your costly richest grain,
In the soul's eternal store-house
   'Twill be gathered up again.

Cast your bread upon the waters,
   Dry the tear from childhood's eye,
Speak a gentle word of comfort
   To the beggar passing by.

Cast your bread upon the waters,
   Hear the outcast's awful moan,
Down into their depths of sorrow—
   Let your love be freely sown.

Benisons of souls in anguish
   Shall ascend to Heaven's high dome,
When the " Master " says Come higher,
   They'll be written on His Throne.

Oh, the bread shall all be gathered,
  For there's not so barren ground
But that if the seed be planted,
  There shall be a harvest found.

To the widow and the orphan
  Wheresoe'er distress is known,
Be it in the gilded palace—
  On the wayside or the Throne—

Be it clothed in purple vestments,
  Or in rags, 'tis all the same,
Every word that giveth comfort
  Is the bread and golden grain.

And the spikenard and the ointment
  Which to use were thought not meet,
They were far less costly offerings
  Than the tears which washed His feet.

And the widow with her offering,
  Though it be an humble mite,
It shall be of greater value
  Than the sacerdotal rite.

And the man who loves his neighbor,
  Be he e'er so rich or poor,
He shall surely find acceptance
  As a good and faithful doer.

And the Book wherein is judgment
  Which the final die shall cast—
That shall gauge our Hell or Heaven
  Will be the retrospective past.

Each one's soul shall be the angel
  That records the deeds they've done,

And so legible be written,
    They shall live when fades the sun

Yes, the Book of Life shall open—
    It shall be the living soul,
And each page whereon is written,
    Will be a true and faithful scroll.

Mountains then shall fail to hide us,
    Subterfuge to fitly screen,
Honest, earnest soul-endeavor
    Alone can wash the spirit clean.

WINE IS A MOCKER.

In the cup of subtle pleasure a thousand furies kindle the altar of their sacrifices on the burning elements of the soul's discomfiture, and, with the cunning sagacity of a vulture, swoop down into the sanctuary of man's strongest citadel, stealing away the proudest emporium of his manhood, leaving but the wreck of a desolated temple on which God had put the signet of his approbation. So inductive are its machinations that the wisdom of the sage has been pronounced against looking upon, touching, or tasting the seductive thing.

At the marriage feast, where holiest vows are pledged, it associates itself in the convivialities of the occasion, concealing in its fruits of pleasure a terrible holocaust that may eventually consume upon its altar all the promised hopes and brightest prospects of this new elysium. In the halls of state it presents its fascinations, kindling the eye and firing the brain with a new enthusiasm, as eloquent and grand in its effect as it is subtle to destroy.

The first cup which bedews the lip with its nectar may be the cloud whose magnitude shall assume proportions as vast as the area of one's mortal existence. Yea, it may bridge over into the hereafter, requiring the majesty of the Infinite to bid its hideousness depart into everlasting darkness, leaving to be mourned by angels the wreck of its machinations. Fair woman, the right hand and queenly support of man, with the sublimity of her exalted and symmetrical nature, bearing the ancient royal high crown of chief workmanship of Jehovah, has been assailed in all the purity and strength of her God-like being by this insidious foe; and, like withered leaves, has fallen from the places she once graced and glorified, to join the lamentable ranks of the riotous caravan which move in the wake of the still. The faces that once rejoiced at her coming, blanch with fear at her approach, and the places that once knew her, know her no more forever. The child, sweet plight of love, who fondled in her caress, and carolled its glee upon her bosom, shudders at her name. The fond husband, who doted upon a trusting, loving wife, laments her in the desolation of her glory, in the despoilation of wife and mother. Oh, sisters, daughters, wives and mothers, that cup of sparkling Burgundy, the exhilerating champagne, has in it a fiend more deadly than the effects of the Upas! It contains in it vials of wrath as terrible as the seven seals.

From out of it shall issue scorpions that shall sting

with terror the immortal spirit. It is the foe, than which there is none other so much to be dreaded, so carefully to be shunned. No pool of Siloam can cleanse its leprous spots ; no healing stream can wash its record clear ; no Christ can be its propitiator ; Heaven has set its fiat against it, and the curse of the Infinite consigns it to outer darkness. It is a foe, the stench of whose crime reaches unto Heaven. It assails the souls whom God has created. It is the despoiler of all that is emblematic of truth, wisdom, purity, excellence and love. It tears man down with its pinched fingers of death, from his high estate of sonship to God ; reduces him to squalid spiritual, intellectual and moral beggary ; transforms the proud, kingly elements of his manhood beneath the degradation of the swine, and in loathsomeness renders him more disgusting than the serpent which God consigned to crawl on his belly all the days of its life. Of all fiends it is the arch one, that goes to-day " up and down the earth seeking whom it may devour," and in the subtleness of its deceit assails the sanctuaries of Heaven, and would wrest from the very treasury of Jehovah the costliest gems created to emblazon His coronet. For its despoilation what has it to offer ? Naught but room for another victim. The insatiable maw of its foul desires are ever crying, Give ! give ! And there comes from yonder tombless mound a warning, muteless voice, " Beware of the wine when it giveth its color in the cup." From the culprit trembling 'neath the halter which is to send his soul unbidden into the presence of its Creator, there to answer for a crime perpetrated under the bewildering influence of this matchless fiend ; from the vacant seats of legislative halls, where once was heard the silver rhythm of the voice of oratory that thrilled with admiration and awe the enrapped listener with its inimitable flow of musical cadences ; from the bar, the absence of the dead counsellor, whose pleadings caused the stalwart frame, and stoutest heart to tremble, and wet the bronzed cheek with tears from eyes long unaccustomed to weep—all these send forth in speechless eloquence, Lo! how are the mighty fallen by the bewitching allurements lying latent in the fascinations of the wine-cup. Who shall answer before that God who judges impartially, for the debauchery of the midnight carousal ? Or who, in the final summing up of the trial which shall adjudge the acts of each one's life, shall be held responsible for the crimes which bereave innocent ones of their natural protectors ?

It may be she who is the proudest ornament of prince- ly palaces, and the devotee of fashionable sociabilities of the most cultured and refined of modern society, whose bejeweled hand unwittingly proffers to him who is to be the future guardian of her happiness in the glass of sparkling champagne the insipient elements from out which shall issue the fell destroyer that shall blight with a deadly blast all their prospects on the voyage of life so auspiciously begun, and bring them both down to the sorrows of an untimely and dishonored grave ; leaving no memories behind them, save those, the rec- ollection of which shall cause the flushed cheek of friends to tingle with sorrow and shame. Perhaps the doting mother, who offers to her son of yet infant years sips from out her cup of toddy, may stand before God as the condemned culprit, responsible for the blackening crimes her debauched son has perpetrated

under the influence of liquor, the uncontrollable appetite having been acquired and fostered by the indulgence of a loving and unsuspecting mother. The ignorance with which the seeds of a holocaust are sown, renders not the fire less destructive.

No longer is the sin of ignorance winked at, and its dreadful effects are mowing down with a remorseless swath, the most promising and brilliant of our land.

The gospel of an enlightened, orthodox, temperance salvation, is as vastly needed to-day in the church as its effects are wanted outside the pale of its sanctuary ; and if a Redeemer should be sent to this world from the distant vaults of Heaven, methinks his beneficent mission would be to promulgate the salutary gospel of total abstinence. So glaring have become the crimes induced by the use of alcholic drinks, so aggressive is its warfare against the best good and morals of society, so insidious in its effects upon the intellectual, moral, spiritual and physical being of those who indulge in its use, that an illuminated pronunciamento against it should be inscribed on the lintels of the doors and windows of the residences of all order-loving citizens.

On the chancel of churches, side by side with " Holiness to the Lord," should be inscribed in golden characters, " Wine is a mocker, strong drink is raging, and whosoever is deceived thereby is not wise." At the entrance of every avenue of the heart, crowning each page of the affectional nature, and on each lintel of the chambers of the soul, should be suspended a flaming sword, forever to wage a holy warfare against the improper and unholy use of this, the most destructive element that now thrusts itself broadcast upon our land. The curse of intemperance seems to me like the forbidden fruit, of which in the day that one partakes they shall surely die, save only as God, by His divine interposition, may in mercy wrest them from the grasp of this fatal adversary of both body and soul. At the wicket gate, where King Alcohol gains admission to set up his demoniacal kingdom in God's earthly temple, I would station in active force, fully armed and equipped, all the battalions of the will power, which with the aid of Almighty God are able to withstand any foe from without. The active use of each faculty of the will to resist temptation of any kind increases its objective force a hundred fold. The effect of intemperance is to cast both soul and body into everlasting fires, such as are only fitted for the devil and his angels; and to this declaration what man or woman, who has felt its flames kindling stomach, brain and soul with its consuming fires, would not give his or her hearty attestation? To lull the insatiable demands which the fires of liquor kindle, the poor, helpless victim cries, "I must have rum! give me rum!" each draught of which adds a new invoice of devils to the legion already rending his poor, distressed physical and spiritual shipwrecked soul and body. What has King Alcohol to offer in compensation for this sacrifice to the dignity and nobility of manhood? And what does he offer to woman in recompense for her fall, and her worship at his shrine? What Satan offered to Christ, if he would fall down and worship him—all the kingdoms of the earth? By no means. This casked-up, bottled and labelled modern Satan, for worship and kinship to him, offers: First—Dethronement of manhood, alienship from God; and, as a rule, robs of earthly treasure, clothes the soul with horror and dismay, and leaves his victim, in the misery of his despair, to call wildly but fruitlessly upon the rocks and mountains of forgetfulness, to hide him from the presence of the condemning judge of an outraged conscience, from the maledictions of which there is no escape. The demoniacal, consuming fiend has taken up his habitation in the soul, his deadly fangs have pierced the spirit, and when his victim would escape him, he thrusts him down and rends him—the power of the Omnipotent ·alone being able to put forth an arm, all-powerful, to save. For a healthy body, costly garments, and a goodly habitation, he compensates by ingrafting the system with the germs of disease, which shall only die out of the being with the dissolution of the mortal frame—not until it shall have been resolved back to earth, and have received her purifying process shall there be exterminated from it the marks and effects of this unmitigated, unrelenting destroyer. In exchange for purple and satin, he clothes his devotee with rags, if so be he even leaves rags with which to clothe. For comfortable habitations, he turns out his bloated and disfigured subject to lie down with the swine (the companions with which his majesty, in a more ancient time, took his bath in the sea). Would to God he had not resurrected himself from the ocean's briny depths. Possibly, upon the drowning of the swine, he took up squatter sovereignty in the whales, and they, preferring to maintain their own individual sovereignty, spewed him out, like his predecessor, upon dry land, to inflict a double curse upon humanity, for the short immunity they had received from his satanic kingship. ·

The victim of alcohol becomes prodigal of all that

is endearing in life, or of good repute. The affections of wife, the love of children, the prayers of parents, the tears of once idolized sisters, to him are as " sounding brass and tinkling cymbals." Yea, the lessons of Calvary, its crown of thorns, the bleeding side of the Crucified, the bitter groans and sweat in the garden, the midnight prayers in Gethsemane, and the last prayer of the self-sacrificing, anointed One, (" Father, forgive them, they know not what they do ") to them who tarry long at the wine, are as " pearls cast before swine."

For mechanical purposes and as a medicine, spirituous liquors have their righteous and proper uses. So have the deadly night-shade, arsenic and strychnine, to cure diseases as fatal as themselves could inflict. But pray, what modern belle of society would think for a moment of offering to her sweetheart a decoction of strychnine, to enliven his spirits for an evening's entertainment? Or what judicious mother would venture to give to her daughter a dose of arsenic, to improve her complexion and give brilliancy to the eyes? Or who would, on New Year's day, present to their guests a libation of opium or of night-shade? That might be done if there were no law against it, and the host did not desire to receive his guest on the return of the next festive occasion. Yet these are not more dire in their effects than the glass of wine with which fond mothers permit their children to toy. The former speedily kills, and throws the pall of death over its victim ere it degrades. The latter leads on by a thousand snares to inevitable ruin and disgrace. Says the Rev. Newman Hall, of New York, a gentleman of high social standing, marked ability, scholastic manners and acquirements : " The Church of England within the last three years has lost in membership by drunkenness thirty thousand." With this fact staring the clergy in the face, the church sanctions the use of the first rounds in the ladder to drunkenness by proffering fermented wine to the lips of the communicant in memory of the spilt blood of Christ. There should be an act of Legislature in each State requiring manufacturers and dealers to label their casks, flasks, demijohns and bottles of champagne, whisky and brandy, as are other less destructive articles of merchandise, with the word " Poison, " in legible characters. The local authorities protect the public against the contagious disease of the leper. The infectious disease of smallpox is regarded of sufficient moment to be brought under the jurisprudence of municipal authority ; while the contagion with which spirituous liquors is sweeping down with a mighty swath of death thousands yearly to an untimely and dishonored grave, is rocked with safety in its infectious cradle by the silence of executive authority. The devastating influence with which alcohol is sweeping like a mighty holocaust over this fair land, the debauchery and drunkenness of young men in the various grades of society, is attributable in a great measure to the license that ladies give to its abominable use as a beverage. Adam was an ungallant bridegroom, but I have no doubt he had occasion, as have modern husbands, to stand unveiled in the presence of their God and say, " The woman that thou gavest me, she tempted me." I doubt not Eve, like her more modern sisters, was comely, and there was some excuse then as now for Adam's shirking responsibility. How many wine-bibbers would there

3

be to-day if ladies would invariably ignore its use, and refuse to receive the attentions of those who should quaff its nectar? Why, it would not be one year before grog-shops would all be closed, and drinking would be as unpopular and less common than employees making appropriations for their own use, from the Government's till. Barley, wheat and corn would find their uses in bread, and the product of the vine would be appropriated to its proper use. The moral influence that ladies could exert in staying the tidal wave of drunkenness that is sweeping back to the ocean of death the brightest hopes of this promising land, would be far more powerful to save than is the allied power of alcohol to destroy. Even were its force quadrupled an hundred fold, it would then fall powerless before the irresistible influence of woman. The husband, father, brother or lover, though they may be valiant in battle, and of heart impervious to fear, yet of all creatures which God has created they are the weakest, when the battle is waged against the loving affections of the woman whom they adore. They are led by her, yield to her and obey her loving mandates. The only fortifications that guard the domestic circle and render it secure, are the bulwarks of love, and its ramparts are the welcoming smile, the cheering word, kindly attentions and the tender caress. Ladies, these are the weapons with which God your Father has panoplied your soul and walled you round. They are the flaming swords which are to keep out from your earthly elysium discord and drunkenness, with the gloomy train of its horrid consequences. These womanly graces and tributes of love are the anathemas before whose divine presence the evil spirit embodied

in alcohol, will coweringly hide away into the shades
of forgetfulness, leaving you in full possession of the
mansion of love of which its owner had accounted
you its worthy occupant. In arraigning the culprit
(drunkenness) for trial before the tribunal of an impartial judgment, while we do not altogether exonerate
the felon, still we charge in a great measure the responsibility of the crime upon the indifference with
which ladies regard the foul offense which steals upon
its victim while he is yet unaware. In the economy
with which God has provided for the government of
mankind, He has so ordained that the stronger
should be sustained, influenced, governed and con-
trolled by the weaker. Woman, by the delicacy of
her persuasion, by her example and affectional nature,
has from the beginning of time been the emperor of
man. While he courts her favor, he bows at her mandates, and becomes her willing, unconscious slave.
She rules his heart, sways his judgment and controls
his actions, in the savage as well as in the civilized
breast. In the fiery heat of his passion she looks upon him, and the hand raised in wrath to slay falls
powerless at his side. As examples of these facts, I
quote the name of the Queen of the North American
Indians, Pocahontas, and the unlettered girl of France,
Joan of Arc.

> Where is the stalwart heart so stout
>   But that to woman bows?
> Or where the will howe'er so bent
> But by the power of women lent—
> On her high, holy mission sent,
>   Finds a redeeming clause?

But what shall we say for the moral status of those in authority, who, for the paltry sum of a few dollars added to the coffers of a city treasury, will legalize the crime of dealing out to human beings potations of distilled death and swift destruction on nearly every street-corner, and flaunt its glaring, high-handed crimes even under the shadows of the sanctuary, whose chiming bells and stalwart towers proclaim, " Holiness to the Lord, and good will to men." Are these the guardians of the peace, and the executors of the municipal government? For what, then, is there to hope? Is the government in the hands of a thoughtless rabble on election days ? Where are the vast army of church members, who subscribe in their tenets of faith to orderliness and sobriety ? Where are the myriads of order-loving citizens, whose ballot should be cast in favor of the best interests of the people at large ? Does familiarity with crime render it less obnoxious to them, and the stench of its filthiness less unsavory, that they roll it as a sweet morsel under their tongue, while they cry, "A little more sleep, a little more slumber, a little more folding of the hands to sleep," that they may withhold their hands from the ballot which shall close these gates of hell, and the entrance to the jaws of death ? When God shall gather up his jewels, how hardly shall these order-loving, responsibility-shirking, church-going citizens be saved ? As the vast army of inebriates pass in review before His throne, will not the Lord of the harvest of tares and wheat say to unrighteous voters : " Inasmuch as ye failed to preserve the sanctity of your high trust, and save these men, by your ballot, from the terrible curse which has befallen them, ye have done it unto me." As terrible as was the fate that befell Sodom and Gomorrah, shall it not be " more tolerable for them in the day of judgment than for these ? " The people of to-day are enlightened, and before Heaven's high tribunal they cannot put in the plea of ignorance. The influence of the earnest prayers and executive acting of high-minded, noble-hearted women have closed the doors of thousands of rum shops from Maine to the Pacific; and the ballots of the stronger sex have opened up again these infamous sluice-ways to poverty, shame, and an ignominious death. What is the result ? Riotous excesses reel their putrescent forms where thrift and happiness had assumed their honored sway; homes are laid waste of love and affection. Drunkenness, with its squalid train of crimes, stalks boldly forth to cast their darkening shadows on the horizon of our beloved land.

There is more potency of hell in spirituous and malt liquors than have been reserved for all the other forces of damnation with which sin has sought to drag humanity down to perdition. Its effects are to cripple the capacities of the intellect, palsy the powers of the soul and demoralize the functions of the physical system. It transforms the image of God in man into a fiend, and imbrutes those who indulge in its hellish nectar. According to the census of the Internal Revenue Reports, it is costing our people a yearly expenditure of over one billion five hundred million dollars.

It is making yearly one hundred and thirty thousand confirmed drunkards.

It is sending yearly about one hundred and fifty thousand to drunkard's graves, and reducing to beggary two hundred thousand children.

It is sending yearly to prison one hundred thousand persons.

Is not this report sufficient to engage the interest of every philanthropist, and secure the attention of every lover of humanity?

The drunkard attempting to reform is fighting a battle such as only a god might expect to win.

In his brighest moments, when the victory seems nearly won, how often do we see him, like the sow that was washed, return to his wallowing in the mire. O young man! as you value happiness, honor and manhood; as you cherish her to whom you have given your heart's holiest affections; as you regard the memory of her who gave you birth, and by your hopes of immortal bliss, forswear thy soul against the intoxicating cup, and for the benefit of those who shall come after you, swear your anathemas forever against it, lest it shall be the "Bridge of Sighs" over which your friends shall mourn your helpless and lost condition.

Oh, proud and exalted man, to whom the government has entrusted, by reason of the ballot, the guardianship of the best interests of the country, the happiness of the people, and the sanctity of the domestic circle : if the righteous shall scarcely be saved, how can you expect to escape the condemnation of Heaven? What subterfuge shall have power to hide you from the condemning judgment of your own soul, in the day when the spirits of men shall stand undressed before the tribunal of their own conscience, and the searching eye of an impartial God ?

Our Country as it Was and Is.

In the primeval morning time,
　　There nature's quiet breast
Lay in its virgin solitude,
　　Unbroken in its rest.

And no response from woodman's ax
　　Was heard in wood or glade,
The soil, unbroken by the plow,
　　Or by the gardener's spade.

The hills had slept in quiet mood
　　The glade and plains among,
No clash of warrior's arms had there
　　Among their fastness rung.

The birds, in sweetest, softest notes
　　Their melody prolonged,
The Eagle from its dizzy height
　　Shrieked out its clarion song.

The restive bear fawned with her whelps
　　In playful, sportive glee,
The sighing water's virgin breast
　　Rolled silvery to the sea.

The Indian roamed in stealthy quest
　　For game and antlered deer,
While not a thought e're stirred his breast
　　That savored of a fear.

The prairies with sweet incense fanned
　　The early morning air,

The daintiest gifts that nature planned
  Sent up their voiceless prayer.

And in her virgin solitude
  She wafted o'er the seas,
The incense of her flowery plains
  On pulses of the breeze.

Columbus caught the cycling wave
  By inspiration given,
And triumphed o'er contending fate,
  And made our shores his haven.

The van of Empires set its sails
  Our country to explore,
And plant the ensign of the cross
  That Indians might adore.

Another band thereafter came,
  They were of sterling worth.
Yet persecution drove them from
  The land that gave them birth.

And here they built their council fires,
  On Plymouth's solid rock ;
Religion was the basic law
  Of that illustrious stock.

The holy treaty—pledge of truth—
  By Penn, and Indians given,
Was like unto the law of Faith
  Twixt man and Courts of Heaven.

The sacred pledge inviolate,
  How firm the treaty stands,
And peace and friendship—heavenly link—
  Was monarch in the land.

One hundred years! stupendous march,
    The song of Freedom sung,
Since *honest* men for liberty,
    Broad-cast their ensign swung.

Then came the conflicts, carnage, strife,
    Of revolution fame,
Right royally was then acquired
    A patriotic name.—

Theirs was a purpose grand and true,
    For liberty and right,
For *this*, they sacrificed their homes,
    For this, they dared to fight.

For this, the clarion sound of war
    Rang forth with accents shrill,
For this, the roll of liberty
    Was called at Bunker Hill.

For this, brave Warren fearless fell
    In battle's hottest strife.
For this, the noble Captain Hale
    Laid down a hero's life.

For this, the dreadful Valley Forge
    Lay crimsoned in its snow,
And blood of noble patriots
    Did copiously flow.

And heroes breakfasted on fares
    Such as a beggar scorns,
For this, they breasted heat and cold,
    And slept in sleet and storms.

For this, the women also toiled,
    Their zeal undimned by gloom,

More earnest plied the busy wheel,
　The needle and the loom.

Their little ones were cradled then,
　In agony and fear,
While terror chilled each mother's heart,
　And froze the starting tear.

But liberty their efforts crowned,
　And valor set them free ;
Long live the memory of the day
　When they destroyed the tea.

Our Country in its rapid growth,
　Full populous we see,
And enterprises ply their arts
　To th' music of the free.

Where roamed the Indian in his quest
　Through glade and forest wild,
There now is heard the song of mirth
　From many a happy child.

And where prime nature sang alone
　Her symphonies of praise,
There now is heard the harmonies
　Of nation's tuneful lays.

And in our Country's amplitude
　She offers on her soil
A full, a free and lib'ral home,
　Just recompense of toil.

The mountain fastnesses reveal
　Their stock of hoarded gold,
And mines of vast intrinsic wealth
　Their stores to us unfold.

The industries set up their art
  On mountain top and plain,
And faithful nature in response
  Yields up her golden grain.

We have in the mechanic's skill
  The sciences combined,
And proofs of progress of the age
  In our inventions find.

In surgery and medicine
  We rank as first in place,
With those who in the medic skill
  The art of science grace.

Our press, untrammeled in its use,
  Has grand achievements wrought,
And still its broad, gigantic power
  Dilates the world of thought.

Our commerce traffics on all seas,
  Its boundaries o'er all lands,
Nations with admiration see
  The power its strength commands.

Steam with its power plies on the wastes,
  Our monarchs of the main,
And subtile air comes in for share
  Her honors to maintain.

And men seek in aerial height
  A power to gravitate
Midway between the heaven and earth
  In equipoise of state.

Our railroads span from shore to shore,
  While lightning binds the main,

And Nations evermore will sing
  For Morse his proud refrain.

Our cities all along the line
  With manufactories teem ;
Up rise our church spires, lofty domes,
  Inthroned in dazzling sheen.

And schools of academic art
  Now grace our fair domain ;
The East, the West, the North, the South,
  Join in the loud refrain—

Of wisdom, excellence and love
  To Him who from on high
Doth trace each Nation in its reign,
  And casts its final die.

The harmonies of chiming bells
  Proclaim our day of rest,
Millions of earnest worshipers
  Its sanctity has blessed.

Societies of Brotherhood
  Fraternal clasp the hand,
And are a strong, protecting link
  Throughout our glorious land.

Their temples rise in lofty towers,
  To Solomon date back,
For charities and noble deeds
  They have indeed no lack.

Religions here from Church and State
  Receive a sanction wide,
While education full and free
  Walks stately by its side.

Our statesmen have been men of mark,
    And sterling, strong, and true;
When discord shook the Ship of State,
    They saw her safely through.

Our clergy, poets, artisans,
    Distinction have acquired—
Their oratory, song, and art,
    Scholastics have admired.

Our Washington, and Lincoln, too,
    Bold champions of right,
Their names will ever thrill the pulse
    Of Nations with delight.

Our jurists have, with wisdom, shown
    Their knowledge of just law,
And set the Constitution right
    Wherein it had a flaw.

Our Army and our Navy, brave,
    Achieved an envious fame,
And History's eventful page,
    Enrolls each gallant name.

Beneath our country's pillared fame
    A serpent's deadly coil
Lay silent in our Roll of State—
    A monster to despoil.

Its circling, grasping, hideous form
    Had been the people's pet;
'Twas handled with the softest touch,
    A Nation's fears beget.

But on that pyre our sacrifice,
    Undaunted, undismayed,

By North and South most precious lives
  As offerings were laid.

Convulsions shook, like Sinai,
  Our country and its pride,
Ere Justice gave the final stab,
  From which the Monster died.

Our soldiers' Decoration Day!
  We spread a floral pall
Both for the North and South alike—
  Our Country lost them all.

Here let us bridge the chasm o'er
  Of fratricidal strife,
And stronger bind the welded link*
  Which guards our Nation's life.

Our Country's glorious jubilee
  Throughout the welkin rings ;
Imperial powers and dynasties
  Their off'ring to us brings,

Historic Independence Hall,
  With wide, extended courts,
Makes room for all the Governments,
  To contrast their reports

With what a fair Republic 's gained,
  Since Seventeen Seventy-six.
How Progress crowns each effort made
  That 's set in Freedom's niche.

Now, Freedom reigns o'er all the plains
  Throughout this vast domain,

---

* Justice and Freedom.

The forge has turned to pruning-hooks
  What once were galling chains.

Our flag now waves, in ampler folds,
  In every land and sea—
Midst shot and shell has reigned supreme,
  Ensign of liberty.

Oh, eagle ! rise on loftiest wings,
  Ring forth the tuneful lyre,
Till Freedom's glorious harmonies
  Each nation shall inspire.

Till Liberty, as free as thought,
  In equity shall reign,
And Truth and Science build a forge
  To weld the golden chain.*

Is Man Intrinsically Evil ?

No! In silver-tongued eloquence comes forth the response from all the primal elements of God's creative power, lying latent or in active operation in animate or in inanimate organism.   For, as in the progress of creation, the Great Artificer reviewing each of his created works pronounced them " very good," who shall best pass judgment—the clay or the Potter who fashioned the clay ?

Every passion of man's soul, every element in his organism, every impulse in his nature, is as pure and

---

* Liberty and Equity.

holy in its intrinsic merit, as the blush that painted its first kiss on the primeval morning sky.

Love and its corresponding demands met in the gratification of its indulgencies are the crowning glory of the essential elements of humanity.

And the mighty Architect, in fitting up this world for the habitation of man, had in view the justice of the demands in physical organism.

And creation shows how beautifully, harmoniously and wisely God has provided for their adjustment.

We are so fashioned as to demand and relish food, and the gratification of this commandment written upon the organism, supplies nutriment for human continuance.

We love water, and its indulgence aids in supplying the fluids of the system and in promoting the general health. We love air, and without its support we perish directly.

We love the light, and the answering of the requisition of this demand unfolds to us the beauties and harmonies of God's created works.

We enjoy the shady night, and in its infoldment we derive that recuperation so essential to sustain the nervous energies.

We are sensitively alive to the delicious fragrance and enchanting beauty of flowers, and in gratifying this passion of the soul our habits and tastes are lifted up through the sublime to the artistic decorations of our houses, gardens and homes.

We love the opposite sex of our kind (" Male and Female created He them ") and by the fulfillment of the commandment — irrevocably written in humanity's soul, and stamped upon every fiber and tissue of its finely and delicately attuned organism, arid wastes and fertile plains become populous, cities rise up in magnificent splendor all over the land, industries, arts and science flourish, religion receives its base on which to build its sacerdotal structure, and Heaven itself teems with spiritual intelligences, having come up through the human organism in fulfillment of the first commandment that went forth to man upon the warm breath of Jehovah.

While I recognize the justice of the claims of all physical demands, I would have their clamorings ascend the scale of intelligence, and sanctified by the *oneness* of love, sit enshrined amid the spiritual and intellectual regions of the brain, the trio acting as umpire over head and heart.

The apparent evil and misshapen developments of Humanity are the results of the misapplication of the footprints of Divinity so subtly infused into the intrinsic essences of humanities spiritual and physical organism.

Sensibilities of pain, apprehensible through our mental, affectional and bodily organism, arouse in us the elements of defense and of self-preservation, the misapplication and perversion of which would amount to ostensible antagonism to the very law we desire to preserve, and men would become unjustly aggressive in the misappropriation of a wise benefaction. And thus it is to be seen, man is *not* naturally evil : he is only so by perversion of natural laws.

The bridle by which the steed of human impulse, passion, inspiration and desire may be properly reined *is* the Mighty Commander of the universe, and no other power can entirely control and develop the hu-

4

man soul and marshal all its capabilities so as to develop in perfect symmetry the beauty of its intrinsic merit.

Harmony of Spirit and Matter.

The harmony of human souls is like a river, whose perpetual flow winds on together into the ultimate sea of each one's spirituality; whose terminus is the exhaustless ocean of spiritualized intellectuality; whose fountain is the fathomless storehouse of infinity, rendered capable of eternal and limitless progression by reason of the constant influx of the centripetal spirit, which creates, and naught can destroy; which wills, and revolving worlds obey; which looks, and foaming seas become as gentle as a rill; which speaks, and wondering hosts stand still; at whose behest stars and planets swell the glad anthem of universal praise; whose echo reverberates through all the vaults of heaven, and sends its cadence of gladness down into the cheerless, rayless, sunless, loveless abyss of woe, till imprisoned souls with wonder see their God, and, joining in the sweet refrain, own " Him Lord of all." Then shall the bridegroom and the bride be indivisible; then shall the " lion and the lamb lie down together," and the child of Truth shall lead them; then shall *Universal* Nature, joining with the morning stars, answer back the refrain as issued from the mouth of Jehovah, " the mornings and the evenings of the eternity of ages behold thy works, and pronounce them very good."

Oh, joy inexpressible,
Oh, bliss ineffable,
Oh, wondrous love divine.

" The heavens Thy glory, Lord, declare—
The earth Thy works proclaim,"
All Nature 's ruled by Thy command,
And glorifies Thy name.

Eternal harmony is Thine,
In heaven, and earth, and sea,
Thy home 's throughout the realms of space,
Thy days—Eternity.

Thou fadest not by length of years,
Nor yet by age grows old,
All time with Thee is as ' twere not—
In Thee all things infold.

Or ever worlds began, Thou wert—
Or fade—Thou still shalt be,
Eternal youth is Thine abode—
Thou fill'st immensity.

Thy chariot 's the universe
Borne on the wheels of time,
Worlds uncreate, at Thy command,
Wheel quickly into line.

From out the vast expanse of space
Thou dost creation bring,
And new-born worlds join in Thy praise,
Thou Universal King.

Thy holy temple 's far beyond
The range of mortal thought,

From out Thy sanctuary, Lord,
 Thou hast creation brought.

There, in that fathomless abyss,
 Thou walkest, Lord, alone,
And whereso'er creation is—
 Thou hast set up Thy throne.

And in the finite realms of space,
 Each grade ascending higher,
Thou hast evolved the human race
 Of which Thou art the sire.

His heart to Thine so well attuned,
 A living, thinking lyre,
Thou canst within his being reign,
 Thou dost his soul inspire.

Upon his brain Thou didst reflect
 The impress of Thy thought,
And thus within man's conscious soul
 Thou hast Thyself inwrought.

And thus through organism came
 The seraphs in their line,
May be it were of finer mould
 That stamped them more divine.

What though the mould were coarse or fine,
 It changeth not Thy plan,
Eternal life Thou hast inwrought
 Through intellectual man.

In his formation Thou hast found
 A substance near akin,
To that within Thy spotless self,
 Free from the taint of sin.

So perfect in his heart attuned
  To that of Thy own lyre,
Thou hast in him an essence found
  Of earth 't is something higher.

And touched by Thy magnetic will
  Responsive to Thy thought,
Blending within his finer parts
  Thou hast Thyself inwrought.

How wondrous is Thy mighty love
  In all Thy works displayed,
In tempest—in the tiny flower,
  Thy glory is arrayed.

Oh! how shall man attempt to scan
  The wisdom of Thy will,
Whate'er of good there is—Thou art—
  May be what seemeth ill.

Or erst the mind can comprehend
  Of Thee the smallest part,
Thou takest up Thy blest abode
  Within the human heart.

Unknown, unseen, yet all around,
  In everything Thou art,
Throughout all time, throughout all space,
  Thou art the greater part.

And yet so subtle is Thy power,
  Thy essence so divine,
Impossible to search Thee out,
  Thy nature to define.

The pearly dew-drop is Thy tear,
  Thou dost descend in rain,

And yet to find Thy biding-place
Man ever must complain.

Thou look'st to us through every star,
Thy voice is in the rill,
It speaks to us in softest tones,
And thunders with it thrill.

We see Thy majesty and power
In worlds revolving round,
In everything by beauty shaped
Thy loveliness is found.

Thy heart of tender sympathy
Pulsates the mortal breast,
And entering into human souls
Gives Thy beloved rest.

HAS REVELATION CEASED ?

The cadences from time past, the inspiration of the present, the mutterings and golden glimmerings of the future, answer, with indisputable, knowledge-laden tongues, No! Great as may have been the ages of the past, science, with its imperial, glittering dawn of the present unfolding of truth, casting its aurora high o'er the mountain tops of a false theology, and into the cavern-vaults of superstition, responds, there cometh other revelations, whose record shall be greater than that which time has rolled back on the scroll of the past.

The pioneers of intellectual, spiritual and moral development, which have long since passed into the eternity of ages, have but broken up the fallow ground for
a greater advancement, wherein is hidden the more
precious germs of truth, to be followed again by those
on whom the dispensation of revelation shall have dif-
fused a more glorious awakening. The tall oaks of
superstition, planted by the hand groping in darkness,
still grasping after light, are, one by one, being up-
rooted by the flaming sword of truth, issuing from the
Eden of divine revelation. Witchcraft and wiseacres
have been supplanted by modern intelligence. The
law of cause and effect has consigned to a resurrec-
tionless tomb the superstitious bigotry of the ancients
Intolerance and religious persecutions have given way
to a liberal and consistent faith; while God the Father,
God the Son, and God the Holy Ghost, are each and
all closely allied to humanity, and see us not afar off;
neither do we look at them as through a "glass,
darkly," but behold them "face to face," through the
marvellous tissues of nature's handy works. "In His
own image created He man, male and female created
He them," and the life or spirit which they inherit,
came it not from the breath of His own nostrils, thereby having created humanity as heirship to a most
royal knighthood, of which God the Father is the
Grand Potentate, and of which each and every member
is approximating a glorious ultimatum in the family of
God, through the revelations of coming ages. God
the Father (eternal Spirit, and first great cause), God
the Son (as manifested in humanity), and God the
Holy Ghost (the soul's sweet Comforter), must forever
remain in communion together: and hence revelations

from Father to child must exist, until, in the culmination of ages, they shall inherit one counsel-chamber together.

The laborers, animate and inanimate, are bursting the charnel houses wherein are imprisoned famishing souls, hungering for more light; and Revelation, clad in imperial robes, fresh from the hand of the Infinite, is proclaiming, " Peace on earth, and good will to men."

The zephyrs waft the glad tidings from the four winds of heaven. The gentle dews and falling rain. with tears of sparkling gladness, tell anew the revelation of love. Each warbling songster is but a heaven-ordained minister, having received the rights of priesthood to sing the songs of universal praise. Each flower, which lifts its face to greet the morning sun, tells the beneficence of that power which creates in love, and despoils but to resurrect in greater glory. Each trembling blade of grass points to the eternal dome from whence naught but goodness flows. Each murmuring brook and bejeweled cascade sigh the requiem of a somber-clad priesthood, and welcome in, as they wind on with musical flow to the sea, the incoming era of hope and intellectual advancement, in which the light of science and spirituality unfold the rich developments of a higher revelation, wherein is seen the manifest wisdom of that universal law of love which creates in wondrous harmony the mighty concourse of heavenly worlds, and fits them up as habitations for the soul on which the signet of immortality has been stamped, and the index-finger of eternal progression has affixed its seal. "God manifest in the flesh " is seen in the kindling emotion of intellectuality, as it radiates the sparkling eye, and reflects itself in the changing countenance, giving expression to the language of thought ere the lips had fashioned its utterance. In acts of kindly benevolence, which give words of cheer to the disconsolate, or smoothes a care from the furrowed brow of age, or gives encouragement to the young aspirant as he struggles up the rocky cliffs in his pursuit after the golden grain scattered here and there from the ripened sheaves of a more advanced harvest, as in every act of devotion in which the developing soul seeks after light from the fountains of truth, may be seen God manifest in the flesh. It is not necessary to go to Jerusalem to receive fresh sources of inspiration or revelation, nor yet to Mount Horeb or Pisgah, nor to the inner temple, where rested the ark of the covenant, in which were deposited the tables of stone, the commandments of the Jewish dispensation; but to that inner sanctuary of the human soul wherein the vulture's eye hath not seen nor the lion's whelps trodden; where God takes up his habitation with humanity; where the tables are ever spread in the living, pulsating temple, ready to receive the commandments and dispensations of revelation which the Omniscient is ever inscribing upon his living tablets. Here is a higher priesthood than was Moses or Aaron, a priesthood which not only has viewed the promised land, but has fitted it up for our habitation, and is now journeying with us, a "pillar of cloud by day and a pillar of fire by night"; and He will surely pass with us safely through the Red Sea and the wilderness of doubt, making sure our passport to the summer land, where our triumphant souls shall bask in the sunshine

of eternal truth, and our feet walk the fields ever
fresh with the budding blossoms, whose fruit withereth
not nor perisheth. but remains an eternal inheritance
for the healing of the nations. Should time complete
its rounds of evolutions. and the scroll of its record
be deposited only in the archives of eternity, and
there should be no more day nor night; still would the
dawning day of new and perpetual revelation be the
light before which all present luminaries would pale
in their luster, and with angel hosts ascribe the bright-
ness of everlasting glory to Him " who is the way, the
truth and the life "; who from everlasting to everlasting is the ever-present revelation of good-will to man.
Every ray of science which sends its divergent flashes
of light athwart the intellectual sky, giving new
sources of delight to the enraptured soul, is but another revelation from Jehovah sent out as a winged
messenger of love from the great store-house of treasures resting in the cabinet of Infinity, every one of
which is a link binding man more closely to his God.

Through revelation we clasp hands with the Infinite ; and as a child, look trustingly and reverently
into the face of our Father. How joyfully we trace
His footsteps in the ages of the past, the music of the
spheres having kept time to His foot-falls.

How eagerly we grasp the hand He so lovingly ex-
tends, and through communion with Him as manifested in the revelation of His works, hold counsel
with cherubims and seraphims, who sung their anthems
at creation's early dawn. Each sea-shell (cloistered in
ocean's briny depths) has, in the drapery of its varie-
gated colorings, fresh developments of a wondrous revelation, and clearly shows, on its canvas-shell, the deli-

cate tracings of an unrivaled Artist. The tiny insect with its meager thread of life, artistically and success-fully building up its temple from the depths of ocean to the crest of its billowy wave, is but planting on coral reef another expression of divine revelation. The mountains, as they lift their formidable heights, piercing the vaults of the eternal blue, resting their heads on the bosom of the sky, as if to approach nearer to the counsel chambers of Infinity, that they might hear the more secret conclave thereof, are but another chapter, in which is penciled by the finger of Jehovah the teachings of his incomparable law. The circling rounds of ages past have inscribed on their tablets of stone, as indelibly as were the command-ments on the mount, the history of their record; and the manifold coverings wove in the loom of incalcula-ble ages, wrapped and interlaced over and around the stony frame-work of earth, are but the canvas sheets, upon whose warp and woof the shuttle of time has written in its thread-work the outgoings and incom-ings of the footprints of Omnipotence; until, by His munificent power, He has brought order out of chaos, and has caused the barren rock to blossom as the rose, and the " Sons of God to shout for joy." Great and incomparable as He is, in the majesty of His creation, and in the manipulations of His law and love; still He claims kinship to earth, and to the inhabitants thereof; holding them in the hollow of His hand, fanning them with the breath of His nostrils, and feeding them from His sumptuous spread tables. The nations lying latent in the womb of future ages will read from chapters of earth and rock our record, as we now read the myste-rious history of the peoples which have preceded us.

Herculaneum, now unveiling herself in the confines of her long imprisoned tomb, is but giving to us a fresh revelation of the wondrous past; and the cloistered womb of earth, now made cavernous by the miner's hand, is lifting the vail from the temple where God had hid away earth's rarest treasures. So science, which is but another name for revelation, is constantly unfolding to our vision the mysteries of God's marvelous storehouse; until, through the agency of revelation, the trinity of intelligence, (God, man and angels) shall sit down and hold sweet counsel together. In the seething tempest which shakes to the very center the superstructure of one's being, the heart lifts its complainings to the Infinite; and though no wail may escape the compressed lips, yet a smothered sigh of anguish pierces the vaults of Heaven, unbars the tabernacle where dwells the source of all compassion, and angels, ever in sympathy with the tender heart of Jehovah, come in response to the call, which binds all intelligence into one great family of unity, to offer ministrations of condolence, and impart their sustaining strength; and man, linking hands with the angels, is enabled to walk, in the dignity of his manhood, upright in the presence of his God. Though the tempest shall howl ever so fierce, still, behind the muttering thunders of a frowning Sinai, watching the swaying tempest, holding in His hand the forked lightning which pierces the spirit, sits a loving Father, directing the storm; and in the deep sea-soundings of the soul, above the roar of the tempest, may be heard, as of yore, the " Master's " voice, bidding the storm in the heart of the tempest-tossed mariner, " be still." The roaring cataract, which bears the spirit down to the whirlpool of despair, hears His voice ; and the billowy waves, rearing their frowning crests mountain high, behold His face, and in abashment backward roll, and pillow themselves on the sobbing bosom of the deep. The winds, rending into shreds the web-work of the soul, see the divine presence, and fold themselves in the shrouds of heaven ; while the nearly-wrecked mariner, loosed from his moorings, like the gigantic iceberg of the North, to be borne down to the gulf-stream, there to he lapped up by the rays of a tropical sun, looks trustingly into the " Master's " assuring face, and walks the swelling breast of sorrow's wave unharmed—secure in the panoply of angels.

A saving Christ walks the wave of Gallilee in humanity's stricken heart to-day, as boldly as He did in the days of a sinking Peter. Moses and Elias are now in as close proximity to earth as when they were seen in transfiguration on the mount ; and God spoke not more audibly to Adam in the garden, than He calls to man in this, the nineteenth century : while angels, in their divine mission, sent out by the Father, walk the earth, clad in the habiliments of men, as really as did the three with whom Abraham conversed ; and in the prophetic teachings of the " wise men " of to-day, the expressions of divine will are as clearly manifest as they were in the earlier revelations given to John on the Isle of Patmos. The Pool of Siloam, touched by the healing virtues of the Eternal, is as efficacious to cleanse the leprous spots, as were its troubled waters when beholding in the embodiment of man that power which spake the dead into life, and caused the scales to fall from eyes hitherto shut out from the light of day.

ART.

Art is the achievement and development of the conceptions of the imagination which the ingenuity of man has reduced to a science and practice, in which are found symmetry of form, elegance of proportion, and the perfection of beauty; the key of which is held in the hand of Omnipotence, who alone is the Master of Art, and from whom all its devices have been borrowed. The schedules from which men draw their designs are spread out on earth and sky; while Infinity works from the limitless canvas-sheet of His own imagery. From time to time He drops a link to earth, by which the ingenious Spirit of Art unravels the beauteous mystery, and with an admiration akin to worship, men pause, and pay profound homage to that which Jehovah hath touched. He distills and draws unto Himself by the magnetic power of His will from the subtle principles of earth and air, the properties with which to paint the sun-beam, and to color the rose. The gray of ocean and the emerald green of forest and meadow-land were inwoven by the chemical shuttle of Divine Art. The pencil and brush which decorates with multiplicity of pictures the plumage of the feathered tribe, are wielded by Him whose goodness lets not a sparrow fall to the ground without His notice. The landscape of hills, plains, mountains, and valleys were sculptured by the artistic chisel of Inflexible Will. A place for the rivers, oceans, and seas was inlaid by the diamond edge of thought, while their waters were made soluble by the kneading of God's plastic hand. The Heavens were builded in their magnificent splendor by the architectural design of Supremacy, and their ever-changing, floating drapery, tinted with unrivaled colors, weaving themselves into fantastic shapes and forms, was the study of Nature's Upholsterer. The conceptions of Raphael and the wild imagery of Doré were but the felt influences upon their sensitive brains of a reflection of the electro-magnetic thought of God, breathed upon their souls as an inspiration, and by them transferred to the canvas a mere copy of Divine Art.

The sublime pictures traced by the poet's fancy, the dreams of Milton, the transition of Dante's fervid imaginings, like the awful scenes portrayed by John on the Isle of Patmos, were but emanations from God, with which they had come *en rapport*. The thought on which the orator takes his loftiest flight, clothing his conceptions with figures whose touch burns into the soul, is but a glimmer of an expression from the endless canvas-sheet with which the Almighty wraps His Majesty.

In Memory of H. C. Kibbe.

Oh, the sad, sad hours of anguish,
   Which rent a brother's heart with woe,
Oh. the galling throes of sadness,
   Which did his noble soul o'erflow.

Crowded around his earthly vision
   Clouds of deadly, darkest hue,
Blotting out each ray of sun-light,
   From his spirit vision's view.

Hope had fled from out its mansion,
  Chased away by trembling fear,
Angels well might weep with pity
  O'er his sad untimely bier.

When the poor came to his notice
  For their wants he freely gave;
When he needed consolation,
  Who was there to help or save?

Happy they who 'scape the burdens
  Which his wearied soul had known,
Happy they around whose pathway
  Flowers with fewer thorns are strewn.

Judge him not, oh erring mortals,
  Heaven alone his jury be;
God discerns the secret impulse,
  Men the outward actions see.

www.ingramcontent.com/pod-product-compliance
Lightning Source LLC
Chambersburg PA
CBHW021516090426

42739CB00007B/637